EXPLAINING
The Amazing Story of Jesus

DAVID PAWSON

ANCHOR RECORDINGS

Copyright © 2015 David Pawson

The right of David Pawson to be identified as author of this Work has been asserted by him in accordance with the Copyright, Designs and Patents Act 1988.

First published in Great Britain in 2015 by
Anchor Recordings Ltd
Synegis House, 21 Crockhamwell Road,
Woodley, Reading RG5 3LE

No part of this publication may be reproduced or transmitted in any form or by any means, electronic or mechanical, including photocopy, recording or any information storage and retrieval system, without prior permission in writing from the publisher.

**For more of David Pawson's teaching,
including DVDs and CDs, go to
www.davidpawson.com**

**FOR FREE DOWNLOADS
www.davidpawson.org**

**For further information,
email: info@davidpawsonministry.com**

ISBN 978-1-911173-29-8

Printed by Lightning Source

This booklet is based on a talk. Originating as it does from the spoken word, its style will be found by many readers to be somewhat different from my usual written style. It is hoped that this will not detract from the substance of the biblical teaching found here.

As always, I ask the reader to compare everything I say or write with what is written in the Bible and, if at any point a conflict is found, always to rely upon the clear teaching of scripture.

David Pawson

EXPLAINING
The Amazing Story of Jesus

As a boy I was brought up in a Christian country. By that I don't mean that everybody in England was a Christian, but it was the only religion there was. Most villages and towns had an Anglican church and a Methodist chapel. There were other denominations, but religious places of worship in England were Christian – though there was one Muslim mosque just outside London. So the choice in Britain on a Sunday morning was: be a Christian or stay in bed! There was nothing much else to do.

Nowadays, if you go to Oxford Street in central London you will wonder what country you are in because we have been overwhelmed with immigrants and we are now truly an international country. So we now have the situation where the religions of the world have come to us and are now living alongside each other. We are just learning as a country how to get used to different religions living side by side.

How are these religions going to settle down with each other? Will they ever settle down?

There are four possible relationships between them. The first is one of *hostility and antagonism*. History has been full of religious wars and a lot of blood has been shed in the name of faith. There have been many struggles between religions – between Islam and Christianity for example, between Hindus and Christians, between different kinds of religion, and even within the same religion. I could give you one instance of the war between Iran and Iraq, which was essentially between two varieties of Islam, the Sunni and the Shiite. Or I could take you to Northern Ireland where Catholics and Protestants have been killing each other until recently – and it is a scandal. Are we going to go on like this forever? Are we going to see endless religious wars in the name of faith? That is one possibility.

The second possibility, which is being tried in various places, is called *separatism*. That means to keep them apart. Eventually it means to have ghettos: one part of the town belongs to one religion and another part to another religion. That is now a feature of English life. There is a little town in Yorkshire called Dewsbury. It has a river running through the middle and everybody on one side is Muslim (even the churches have become mosques) and everybody on the other side is everything else. There are even notices in certain cities in Britain that say "You are now entering a zone of Sharia Law", incredible though that sounds. We are seeing separatism keep the religions apart and then we can keep the peace. "Lock them up in their own ghetto" – that is not the solution.

The third solution is *pluralism*. It is a philosophy that variety is good for a society and therefore you encourage all religions, especially minority religions, and it is supposed to be good for a country. It is based on the idea that all religions are equal, that they are all roads leading to the same god, and therefore we should have them all with us. It is basically called relativism. Each religion is regarded as having some of the truth and therefore we need them all contributing to the pool of knowledge.

The fourth solution is now becoming the most common one, and the Bible predicts it will be the main one before we reach the end of the age. It is *syncretism* – persuading the religions of the world to get together and act together, until there is one religion uniting the whole human race. It has begun to happen in my country. Prince Charles, who will be our next king, should inherit a title of the sovereign of Britain which appears on every coin in our land – "Defender of the Faith". Everybody thinks that is the Christian faith, but he wants to change the vow he takes when he is crowned king. He wants to be known as "Defender of Faith", whatever faith that is. He is already commending other faiths to the British people.

The government now no longer talks about "church" or "churches" but about "the community of faith" and it lumps us all together in that. There is a pressure on us to get together with other religions. The pressure is for the sake of bringing some harmony into the community. Of course the different faiths can't get it together on their beliefs because they vary so greatly that you can never combine them. As far as doctrine goes, all religions of the world could be wrong but only one can be right. But the hope is that we might get the *behaviour* of different religions together. That is why the word "virtues" has been replaced by the word "values". It is on a base of common values that the religions are being pressed to get it together. Already different religions in my country are acting together against social evil. They are acting together against poverty and other social evils – hoping to share the same values. You may not know this, but when Mohammed himself wanted to combine with the other religions that believed in one God ("monotheists"), he issued a call to them. It was a very powerful appeal for other religions to come and join him, entitled "A Common Word". He appealed to those other two religions, Christianity and Judaism, with this common word: "We both love God, we both love our neighbour, why don't we get together?"

Interestingly enough, after a gap of fourteen hundred years, the Muslims have made another appeal with the same title, "A Common Word", and they have issued it to evangelical Christians. The appeal is: "Let's love God and love our neighbour together." Two hundred leading evangelicals around the world have responded positively. This may surprise you, but I dare to name some of them: the late John Stott, Brother Andrew, George Verwer, the leaders of Youth With a Mission, have signed a positive statement sent back to the Muslims, saying: "We are prepared to try and get together to discuss this." So there is a tremendous pressure on all kinds of Christians to syncretise religion, and it will ultimately succeed. There will be a world religion led by a false prophet and the pressure will be on all of us to join.

How do we prepare for that? What is our defence against that pressure? It is growing daily in my country, I believe. My sense is it will grow, and others will also be subject to the same pressure. There is a very simple answer to it all and that is to be sure of the uniqueness of Christ. That is the only thing that we can use to prepare to meet the pressures that will be on us. I am referring to the uniqueness of Christ that makes him quite different. By "uniqueness" we mean that he is one of a kind – there is no one else like him; and that he cannot be compared with any other religion, he can only be contrasted with them.

So I want to go through the life of Jesus and say what is unique about our Lord Jesus Christ, that makes him different from every other religious leader, every other religious founder in the whole world, and will always prevent us from falling for the idea that we can bring our religions together and make them one. Many people have tried this. There is a faith called the Baha'i Faith whose headquarters is in Israel itself. That faith aimed to bring together all religions of the world – those who share the same values. An American statesman called John Foster Dulles incorporated the World Congress of Faiths, which still meets, and that has the same objective. So let us turn from all that to the Gospel stories and learn again what is unique about our Lord Jesus Christ which means we will never be able to mix our faith with any other.

We are going to start with his birth. Actually, Jesus' birth was fairly normal. After some hours of labour, Mary produced a baby boy, and that is fairly normal. The only different feature was that Mary's hymen was pierced by a male from the inside. Usually that happens by a male from the outside at the first act of intercourse. But her male baby pierced the opening to her womb from the inside. Apart from that, Jesus' birth was like everybody else's. You have got to go back nine months before the birth to find what was unique about that birth. You find then that he was born without any intercourse between a man and a woman – it was a virgin birth. Incidentally, even the Muslims believe that firmly about Jesus – that he was born of a virgin who had never had any sex with a man.

Now that is not unknown in history. There have been others. A professor of gynaecology in London University told me that there were at least half a dozen other claims in history for virgin births. He was inclined to accept them for a very particular reason. It happens under a process which the scientists call parthenogenesis. That is when a female egg spontaneously divides and goes on dividing and developing into a foetus, and ultimately into a new individual.

There is quite a lot of parthenogenesis in the plant world. There is also the same in the animal world. I think I was told that the Komodo dragon can do the same thing. But here are claims that it has happened to human beings. The professor told me, "The reason why I'm inclined to believe those claims is that in every single case it was a little girl." That is all it could be, because every egg in a woman's body is female, and a female is quite incapable of producing a male child.

That makes the birth of Jesus, or the conception of Jesus, unique. It seems as if the only way it could have been done was for God to create a male sperm carrying his own DNA, and with that her egg was fertilised. Every other way that has been suggested would mean that Mary was not the mother of Jesus, just an incubator, a foster mother. But Jesus was truly the son of Mary. But it also meant that God would be his Father, and that surely is unique. Nobody else has ever claimed that, but he did.

That is not the only surprising thing about the conception and birth of Jesus. The most startling feature is this: he was the only human being who has ever lived on earth who chose to be born. I didn't choose to be born. You didn't choose to be born. I didn't choose my parents, nor did you. But Jesus did. The amazing thing is that he chose very humble parents in quite a poor home. But again and again he never said, "I was born." He always said: "I came" to do this; "I came to seek and save the lost." He decided to come. That is unique. No other religious leader or founder ever claimed to choose to be born; they were simply born as an accident, as it were, as we all were. But Jesus said, "I came." That is the first great unique thing about Christ which sets him apart, one of a kind, who can't be fitted in to any category.

The surprising thing is that for the most famous person who ever lived we know so little about him. There is nothing about him in the first twelve years of his life. We know nothing except that there was an attempt to murder him very early, which resulted in many of his cousins who were in Bethlehem at the time, being killed. But his boyhood is largely hidden from us until the curtain is pulled aside at the age of twelve. When we see what he is doing then it is quite surprising.

Now every Jewish boy has a Bar Mitzvah. It is a ceremony in which he changes from being a boy to a man. I wish we had such a ceremony today, I think it is a very good idea because it recognises responsibility. A Jewish boy goes to the synagogue and he reads part of the law of Moses, which is saying to the people, "I am now responsible for myself, to keep this law." Up to the age of twelve, Jewish parents are responsible for the behaviour of their children. But at twelve the boy becomes an adult. From that moment he puts away all his toys, he puts away childish things, and then he joins his father in his trade or profession. It seems that they took Jesus not to the synagogue for his Bar Mitzvah but to the temple in Jerusalem. His mother and father travelled with him up to the capital city of Israel.

Now I want to tell you how they travelled. There were no buses, no trains – they walked. This is how they walked: the women set off first with the children under twelve, and they walked fifteen miles each day. When they reached the place where they were going to spend the night they put the tents up, cooked the evening meal, and by the time they had got that ready all the men arrived. Do you like the idea? Feminists don't seem very excited, but that is how they used to walk.

They took Jesus to the temple, gave him his Bar Mitzvah – he was duly given a ceremony – and then they set off walking home. Joseph and Mary walked fifteen miles down towards the Jordan Valley and then met up at evening for the meal. Mary said to Joseph, "Where's Jesus?" Joseph said, "Well he's not my boy, I thought he would be with you." Then they realised that each had thought he would be travelling with the other away from Jerusalem. That explains why they lost him.

They went back to Jerusalem, they searched for three days, and finally they found him back in the temple having an amazing discussion with the priests. Mary, typical mother, said, "Your father and I have been looking everywhere for you! Why did you do this to us? Where have you been?" Now notice what she said: "Your father and I." What did he reply? But I am twelve; I have joined my Father in his business. Didn't you expect that? It must have come as a shock to the parents. They had never told him how he was born or conceived. Mary had kept these things in her heart for twelve years and yet here he is – he knows perfectly well who his Father is. "Your father and I have been looking everywhere for you."

"My Father? I've joined him in his business. You should have come first to the temple; that is where you'd find me."

That is a little glimpse we have of a unique boy who already had a unique relationship with God – called him "Father". His favourite word for God the Father was "Dada" or "Daddy" – because every Jewish baby is taught his first word "Abba" which means "Daddy". You see a Jewish father leaning over the pram looking proudly at his son, and this great big monster face appearing at the little baby says, "Abba, Abba, Abba." Finally the baby, to get rid of this monstrous face, says, "Abba." The father says, "He said it! He has recognised me!"

I remember going on a walk with a father on an archeological site in Israel. The little boy was dragging behind and getting more and more tired. He came running after us with his little hands stretched out wanting to be picked up. I heard for the first time someone say, "Abba, Abba." It is a profound word. Jesus said to his followers that is what you ought to call God. No Jew would ever dare to use such intimacy with Almighty God, when God had said, "Don't take my name in vain."

Well that is his birth which was unique, and that is his boyhood which was unique. Then the curtain comes down again for another eighteen years and we know nothing more.

It is extraordinary that we know so little about Jesus. We presume – because he was called the carpenter later – that he went back to Nazareth. Amazingly, it says, "He was subject to his parents." He then took over the business of carpentry and made chairs, tables, window frames, and door frames. If God had put you in charge of planning the life of his Son to be the Saviour of the world, I will guarantee you would have arranged meetings, crusades, and I don't know what else. You would not have put him in a carpenter's shop for eighteen years, but that is what God the Father did.

Jesus was eighteen years a woodworker and three years a wonder worker. If my mathematics are right that is a ratio of six to one. What does that remind you of? He said, "My Father works until now, and now I work." When you turn back to Genesis 1, to God's work of creation, there it is again: six to one. It is interesting that God the Father put his Son to ordinary work with his hands for six years to one year of miracles and message. So that is all we know about this most famous person who ever lived, until the age of thirty. Then he strolled onto the public stage of history and within months was famous for many things. The extraordinary question that is raised is this: after only three years of public ministry he is judicially murdered as one of the worst criminals who ever lived. Every person must try to answer the question: why should such a tragedy happen? Let us look at the unusual features of those three years of ministry to see if we can answer that question.

There are three aspects of what Jesus did in public. The first was his miracles, the second was his morality, and the third was his message. Somehow, for one of those three things he was regarded as the most dangerous man alive, who must be put to death before he did harm to the whole people.

Was it his miracles? Well he certainly did miracles. Do you know that in the records of Jesus outside the Bible we have historians who wrote about him? Roman historians, Jewish historians, not part of the Bible, but they all agree on one thing, that Jesus was a miracle worker. Certainly that is the most attested fact about him.

His miracles divide into two groups: those he did on people and those he did with things, and both are remarkable. The difference is that some of his miracles on people were being done by other people at the same time. He mentions that. He casts demons out of people, but others did that too. He once said to those others, "Why are you accusing me of doing this by the power of the devil? By whose power are you doing it?" So clearly there were other miracles at the time of healing disease and of casting out demons, and he did both.

But the supreme miracle he did with people, which nobody else was doing at the time, was raising the dead. He stopped the funeral of the son of a poor widow. She had only that one son to look after her. He raised the man out of his coffin and gave him back to the widow. That was quite a miracle. But there was a unique miracle he did with a man – a man who was already in his grave and had been there for four days. His own sister said, "We can't open the tomb because he stinks – he'll be rotten by now." Yet he called Lazarus out of that grave, restored a putrefying body to perfect health, and then said, "Take the grave clothes off him. Let him go." That hastened his own death, but not directly. It did make the leaders of the nation (particularly the religious leaders) envious. That was one of the motives that led to his death, but not the main one.

So here is a man who used miraculous power to do amazing things for people and with things – a man who could stand up in a boat and tell the wind and the waves to shut up. He didn't say, "Peace, be still," that is the polite version we have in our Bibles. He actually said, "Get muzzled." It is the way you talk to a puppy dog who is jumping up at you and spoiling your clothes, "Get down!" That was how he spoke to the wind and the waves, and they obeyed him. Immediately the men who were with him in the boat said, "What kind of a man is this, that even the wind and the waves do what he tells them?"

He also changed water into wine. One American pastor tried to tell me he didn't but changed it into tomato juice, but I am sure that is not the truth. He changed it into the best wine at a wedding. They said, "Why have you kept the best wine till last?" because the normal procedure was to give them the good wine at first, and then when they were half drunk pass off bad wine to them. But he gave them the best wine at the end, and he had made it out of water. That is a real miracle with things which nobody else did at the time.

Then also he took two fishes and a few buns of bread and said to the disciples: "There are five thousand people listening to me all day and they have had no food. Why don't you feed them?" The disciples said, "We haven't got anything and there are no shops nearby." Then they found a little boy who had two fish and five little buns of bread for his picnic lunch and the disciples confiscated it. They said to Jesus, "Here's some food we found." For five thousand people? Ridiculous! But Jesus took those two fish and the five pieces of bread and he just kept breaking bits off and giving them to the disciples. "Just take this to the people. Tell them to sit down in groups of fifty. Now take this to them." He was creating that while he distributed it. That is a great miracle.

Then on one occasion he came to a fig tree expecting to find some figs because he was hungry and he had nothing to eat. He found no figs on it so he cursed the tree. Now make of that what you will, but he did it. The next day when they came into Jerusalem by the same path they said, "Look, the tree you cursed. It's dead. All the leaves have fallen. You can see the tree is just a skeleton." Now all these things he did with nothing more than a word, so those miracles were real miracles.

But none of them harmed anyone. All of his miracles did good things for people. That is why, years later, Simon Peter said, when he preached about Jesus, "He went about doing good." Why then should he be put to death within three years for just going about doing good? It is obviously not his miracles that were the problem. So let us move on to the second part of his public ministry: *his morality*. Now you would not dare say to your best friend, "Can you find anything wrong in me?" You certainly wouldn't say to the people that you work with, "I'm humble." Yet Jesus did both and got away with it. He said, "Which of you convicts me of sin?" and he is talking to his worst enemies. Even one of his closest friends, Simon Peter, once said to him, "Depart from me, get away from me! I'm a sinful man! I'm not for the likes of you, I shouldn't be a friend of yours."

It was the testimony of his cousin John the Baptist when he came for baptism. Baptism is to get you cleaned up; it is to wash away your sins. John the Baptist said, "I shouldn't be baptizing you; you should be baptizing me," which means that the first baptist was not baptized. Incidentally, didn't you know that the New Testament called Jesus a baptist? He was a baptist. The same word applied to John, "the baptist", is applied to Jesus on the same page. So there we are—baptists, small "b" not big "B"! But John said, "You're clean. You've nothing to wash away. Why do you come to be baptized?" Jesus said, "It's right to do what is right." Any Christian who is not baptized and says "I don't need to be" needs to remember that Jesus was the only person who didn't need to be, and he was. So follow his example.

John the Baptist said, "You're clean." Peter said, "Depart from me for I'm a sinful man." The enemies of Jesus when he challenged them to find anything faulty in his character were silent. Now the life of Jesus has been more written about, mulled over, examined, than any other life, and no one has found any sleaze, any corruptibility in him, nobody in two thousand years, and they have dug around in his life in detail.

Not only that, but he taught the highest moral standards for other people as well. Everybody who has read the Sermon on the Mount admits that. Like Mahatma Gandhi or the Russian, Dostoyevsky, many a person has said the Sermon on the Mount is the highest moral standard that any teacher has dared to make. The only criticism that people have made of Jesus' moral teaching was that it is too high a standard, that it is impossible to keep. But Jesus was not like many teachers who lower the standards to make it easier for people to reach them. Jesus came to lift people to the high standard, and that was his approach to morality.

Why should they kill a man like that – a person who himself was so moral, and who taught others to be so moral – with the most horrible death there has ever been? That is still the big question. So we must turn from his miracles and his morality to *his message*. There must be something in what he said that caused him to be crucified. That is the truth; that is the answer.

When you look at his message the astonishing thing is that nobody but nobody ever talked so much about himself. In anybody else that would be sheer egotism. A person who is always talking about himself is usually boring. Have you got a friend who always does that? Don't you wish they talked about you? I know one or two people who begin every other sentence with "I" and they are boring people, only interested in themselves. Jesus said more about himself than anybody else, yet he never bored people.

What did he say? Do you know that early in his career they sent soldiers to arrest him and they did not dare to do so? They came back and simply said: Never did a man speak like this man. We dare not arrest him. He is just different. He speaks like nobody else. The simple answer is that – in ten different ways as he spoke about himself – he was actually saying he was God. That is why they crucified him. Let us go through ten hints that he dropped in his teaching which clearly pointed to this extraordinary claim. They knew he was a real human being, but he is actually claiming to be divine, to be God, to be a God-Man. That is an extraordinary claim.

First, as I have mentioned already, he said: *"I chose to be born. I came...."* He even added, *"I came from heaven."* That is a clear claim to be divine.

The second way in which he did it was *his claim to forgive sins*. Now the only sins I can forgive you are the sins you have committed against me. I hope I can forgive that. But Jesus said, "I'll forgive all your sins. All your sins against God, I can forgive them." Well no, a human being can't do that. You can only forgive sins done against you. To forgive a person all their sins against God – you have got to be God to do that, and yet he did it.

The third way was that claim *to have a unique relationship with God*, the only Jew who ever dared to call "Abba" – a very intimate relationship. He never said, "Our Father". He always referred to God as, "My Father" and "Your Father", making a clear difference between his relationship and theirs.

The fourth thing was *to use God's name about himself.* We know the name of God: I Am. Once I asked the Lord, "Could you give me a simple English word that would correspond to your name? I'd like to use it." Quick as a flash into my mind came the word "Always". What a lovely name for God that is. That is what "I Am" means. It is the present tense of the verb "to be". It is not the straight verb "to be", it is saying, "Always I am. I was around at the beginning. I'll be around at the end. I'm always around. I Am." Some people just use the word "being" but I like the word "Always" and I like the name for Jesus which is "Yes". He is the "Yes" to every promise of God.

Fancy having a God called "Always" whose Son is called "Yes". What a positive religion is ours. But he used the name "I Am". He didn't just use the word "I Am", he repeated the word "I" and always said, "I, I Am." In Greek that is *ego eimi*, and *eimi* means "I am" and *ego* means "I". So he began many of his sayings with, "I, I Am... the Bread of Heaven, the Good Shepherd, the way, the truth, the life." Seven times he referred to himself beginning with God's name. They are all in John's Gospel, as it happens.

On one occasion he claimed to the Jews that Abraham was glad to see his day. They said, "You're not fifty years old. How do you know Abraham who has been dead these two thousand years?" He said, "Before Abraham was, I Am." The Jews took up stones to stone him immediately because that was blasphemy. The law of Moses is exactly the same as the Muslim law in this respect: blasphemy deserves death. It is one of the worst crimes a man can commit. We are beginning to understand why he died. So that was number four: he used the same name as God of himself.

Fifthly, he said, *"I am the only way to God. If you want to know God the Father you'll have to come through me."* In a word, he was condemning all other religions in the world. He is saying, "You'll never get through to God the Father unless I help you. Come through me." Now that is an extraordinary claim.

Sixth: *he claimed to be the way, the truth, and the life.* Not *a* way among others or *a* truth or *a* possible life. He kept saying the way, the truth, the life – nobody but God should say that.

Seventh: *he claimed that he would set people free from*

themselves by dying for them. Therefore he said, "I came to die" – he was to die at a very early age. The only thing that kept him from dying was that the disciples had to know who he was before he died so they would see his death in the right light. He took them way up to the foot of Mount Hermon. I hope you will go there someday – it is an extraordinary natural feature. The river Jordan comes out of the foot of Mount Hermon – a full river, straight out. The snow on the top of the mountain melts and it comes down inside a fault in the rock and then it gushes out at the foot of the rock. You might imagine that was a special place, and an especially superstitious place, and so it was.

If you go there today you will see little alcoves carved in the cliff face which held all manner of gods to worship. One of them was the god "Pan" and the locality is still called Panias. The god Pan was believed to be a Greek god who came in the appearance of a man. In another alcove was a statue of Caesar. That is why in Jesus' time on earth the village was called Caesarea Philippi after the Roman Caesar and the local Jewish governor. Here was a man, Caesar, who was a man but who was worshipped as a god.

It was there that Jesus took his disciples and he said, "Now who do you think I am?" Was he the God who appeared as a man or a man who is God? "Who am I?" At first they said, "Well, you're a reincarnation of some great man." That was what other people said. For the first time, Simon Peter said, "I believe you are the Christ, the Son of the living God." He was the first man to say it.

Do you know who was the first woman to say it shortly afterwards? The name is "Martha", who was so good in the kitchen while her sister sat at Jesus' feet. It was Martha who saw the truth of who Jesus was even before Mary. That was the truth. Jesus immediately said, "Now I can die. You know who I am so you will understand now why I am going to die." He clearly indicated that he had decided when to die, how to die, and where to die. He said, "We're going straight to Jerusalem now and I'm going to die there on a cross."

I do not know if you have noticed there were five previous occasions when people had tried to kill him. The first time was in his own village, Nazareth, when he preached his first sermon in the synagogue and they immediately tried to throw him off a cliff. It must have been a good sermon. I have never had that experience. I am amazed that a congregation hasn't thrown me off a cliff when I look at some of the sermons they have had to put up with!

Fancy preaching one short sermon from the prophet Isaiah, and all he said was, "Today you're seeing this happen." Now why did they do that? Were you ever puzzled? What was in that sermon that upset them so deeply? The answer was this. Nazareth is in the northern part of Israel called Galilee. It was a pretty rebellious part, where all the revolts happened and, above all, where all the false messiahs arose who promised to get rid of the Romans. When these false messiahs were put to death, one of the things the Romans did was to destroy the village from which they came in Galilee to prevent any others coming.

That happened in Czechoslovakia when Reinhard Heydrich, the German officer in charge of the occupation, was murdered. Then the Germans took a village in Czechoslovakia just outside Prague and wiped it off the map. It is now a shrine to remember that happening. Well the Romans did the same thing. It was the way they kept messiahs down, killing them and wiping out the village they came from. Here is Jesus claiming to be the Messiah and the whole of Nazareth was scared stiff that they would be wiped out by the Romans. So they said, "Better kill him and not be wiped out ourselves." You can understand it. That was the first time that they tried to kill one man to save a lot of others. Later, Caiaphas said, "It's better for one man to die than that the whole people should perish." It was the same fear of the Romans. In between there were three other occasions when they tried to kill Jesus. But because it wasn't his time he quietly and serenely walked through the crowd and away. But once the disciples knew who he was, he said, "We're going to Jerusalem and I'm going to die."

Eighth: *he promised to come back before his body rotted.* That was a promise God had made way back in Psalm 16, that if ever a holy person walked the earth God would not let him rot in the grave – a very interesting promise which is quoted in the New Testament. That was an extraordinary claim. You see they were going to put him to death because he was too bad to live. He died appealing to a higher court. He died saying: "God will vindicate me; God will reverse your verdict. You will put me out of the world but God will put me back in." When we come to it that is exactly what God did. "I will come back from the dead before rot sets in" would mean before the fourth day.

Ninth: *"I will be the judge of the whole human race. The future of every human being is in my hands. I will separate the entire human race as a shepherd divides the sheep from the goats"* – which means quite simply that Jesus will judge Confucius, Buddha, Mohammed, and every other religious leader will stand before Jesus and he will decide their future. That is quite a thing to say. Pontius Pilate will one day be judged by Jesus. So will Adolf Hitler. So will you and so will I, because he said, "I am the Judge." All the Jews believed that God would judge them, but here is Jesus saying: no, I'm going to do it."

Finally, number ten, he said, *"I will one day return to planet earth for a second time to rule the whole world."*

Now when you put all these ten things together, any one of them wouldn't be enough, but there is a kind of cumulative evidence in those ten things which made it absolutely clear that Jesus was saying he was God.

Now you have only three choices. Jesus was either mad, bad or God; he was either a lunatic, a liar or the Lord. You have got to make up your mind. All human beings have to make up their mind. Either he was deceiving himself and was crazy, schizophrenic or whatever, or he was a bad man deceiving a lot of other people and telling lies about himself – or he was telling the truth. You can't have it any other way. It must be one of those three.

I had a big debate in London in a place called The Inns of Court where top lawyers in London have their offices. We debated: was Jesus mad, bad or God? We had a professor of psychology from London University whose conviction was that Jesus was schizophrenic, that he was crazy. We had the president of the British Humanist Association saying that he was a very bad man and was fooling people with lies. And muggins here had to say that he was Lord. I give the glory to God that we won the debate by eighty-five percent. That is because I had a trick up my sleeve called the resurrection. I will come to that in a moment.

So really Jesus was crucified purely because he called himself God and for no other reason. The first charge laid against Jesus by the Jewish court was that he was blaspheming. Actually they couldn't get witnesses to agree on what he said and it looked as if they couldn't do anything with him. So finally the judge did an illegal thing and charged him to condemn himself out of his own mouth and said, "Are you what you say you are?" He simply said, "I, I Am." The man in charge of the court ripped his clothes and said, "You've all heard it. We've got seventy witnesses who heard him call himself God. What is your verdict?" Sixty-eight of them said, "We vote for his death." That's the only punishment fit for a man who uses those words. But they couldn't put him to death because they were under Roman authority. The Romans had forbidden them to exercise capital punishment so they had to change the charge. By the time they got to the Roman governor, Pontius Pilate, they changed it from blasphemy to treason, that he said he was King of the Jews. That was treason in the Roman law. There was no Roman law against blasphemy, it was a Jewish law. But the Roman law was against treason. That is how they got him killed.

Now there are certain extraordinary unique features of his death. They nailed him to a block of wood stark naked with no loincloth (that is just on the Christian representations for decency's sake). In utter humiliation, stark naked, he is nailed to a cross and left to die. But he didn't die of crucifixion. That is the extraordinary thing. What did he die of? Well, not crucifixion because just to nail a man to a cross and leave him there takes a minimum of two days to kill him, and anything up to seven. That was the range of time it took – the average would be three or four days as he gradually weakened.

What killed a man on a cross was that he suffocated. When his legs became weak and he drooped and hung by his hands the pressure on his lungs would be unbearable. So he would push himself up with his feet again and the agony in his feet would set in and he would flop again. This alternate flopping and pushing himself up is how they died until ultimately they couldn't push themselves up and suffocated. That is crucifixion, the most cruel, slow, lingering death that has ever been devised. No Roman citizen would be subject to it. It was only done to others and only for the serious crimes.

So what did Jesus die of? Well, we know. When by six o'clock in the afternoon they wanted to bury him, the Roman governor sent soldiers to make sure he was really dead. They couldn't believe he was. The only way to hasten death was to use a spear to break the legs, and then the crucified person couldn't push himself up to breathe. So they came to the two thieves and they broke their legs. Immediately they hung and then perished fairly quickly. But when they came to Jesus, to their utter astonishment, he was already dead. But the soldiers had to make sure and they pierced under his ribs with a spear. There came out blood and water. Somebody who was there noticed it and recorded it for us. What does that mean? Well quite frankly it means he died of a ruptured pericardium, or in simple English, he died of a broken heart.

Though he was on a cross and it would have killed him in a few more days, he had died of a broken heart already. Why was that? He had been only six hours on the cross. During those six hours, the first three he was entirely concerned with other people, not himself. He was concerned about the soldiers who put him there and said, "Father, forgive them, they don't know what they're doing." He was concerned about his mother and asked John the apostle to look after her, and John took her to his own home from that moment. He was concerned about the thief dying alongside him, a thief with incredible faith who looked at this dying, naked man on the middle cross and said, "Lord, remember me when you get your kingdom." What faith! Jesus said, "Today you'll be with me in Paradise." So for three hours while the sun shone and the noonday sun was hot and dry he was concerned about others.

But from midday to three o' clock he was concerned for himself. His first concern was simply physical thirst, "I'm thirsty." They cruelly gave him vinegar to drink, which just makes you more thirsty. Then he cried out a terrible cry, "Lama sabachthani. My God, my God, why have you left me?" It is a terrible cry. Through those three hours there was terrible darkness. The sun went down. Just as the star had shone at his birth, now the sun went down at his death. Do you realise what was happening? He was going through an experience of hell. Hell is a thirsty place. It is a lonely place because God isn't there. It's a dark place too – outer darkness, Jesus called it. Jesus went through hell for three hours so that none of us need go to that dreadful place. He was taking our place.

But his final, seventh word from the cross was a prayer he learned at his mother's knee when he was a little boy. Every Jewish boy is taught to pray this goodnight prayer. It is just before he goes to sleep, he was taught to say, "Into your hands I commit my spirit." The only difference from that boyhood prayer that Jesus prayed was to put the word "Abba" in front of it. "Abba, into your hands I commit myself – my spirit." Now that means he was appealing to God to show the world that they had been wrong to put him to death. He knew it was his Father's purpose that he should die, but he also knew it was his Father's will to reverse the verdict before his body had rotted. So he said, "I'll be back."

By the third day he was back eating supper with his disciples, cooking breakfast for them. This was real; it wasn't a ghost. In fact he said, "Handle me and see I'm not a ghost." He came back in a body. However, he left the grave clothes, which had just collapsed, behind in the grave. There was nothing in them, which means that his old body had simply disappeared and God had created a new body for him in the darkness of the tomb. That new body had qualities the old body never had. It could pass through locked doors. It could disappear and appear at will. For the next two months he appeared and disappeared and did both. Why didn't he just come back and stay with them? Because he was teaching them – in the only way that a good teacher could – that they would have to learn to depend on his invisible presence.

So Thomas, one of the Twelve, was not there on the first Easter Sunday evening. They told him he was alive – he has been here. Look! Fish bones on that plate, he ate fish with us!

Thomas said, "You're not going to fool me. No way. Unless I can put my finger through his hands, and put my hand under his ribs, and feel that spear thrust, you're not going to get me to believe." One week later they are in the same room and a well-known voice says, "Thomas, you want to put your finger through my hand, come and do it. You want to feel the scar in my side, you're welcome, come and do it." Thomas never did. He realised in a flash of inspiration and said, "My Lord and my God."

Nobody but nobody has ever come back from death after three days. They have been recovered from death. I have a friend in America who was dead for ten days and Christ raised him from the dead. He was a good pastor. One day he developed a bad pain in the bottom of his back. When he went to the doctor, he said, "You've got a cancerous growth in your spine. It is a very dangerous operation to remove it – I'll try, but no guarantees." He tried having painkillers, and he became addicted to those drugs. Finally, one night he was so desperately in pain that he got hold of a gun, which he had in the drawer of the bedside cabinet, and he went through to the bathroom in his wheelchair, put the gun to his head, and pulled the trigger. There were bullets in every hole except one and he pulled the trigger against that one. It just brought him to his senses and he wheeled himself back to the bedroom and told his wife what he had done. He said, "I can't bear this pain."

"Well," she said, "you'd better go and have the operation. Better to run the risk of getting better or not than blowing your brains out."

So he went. In the hospital he read a verse from one of the early Psalms which said, "I go to sleep and I wake up for the Lord is with me." He wrote that on a piece of paper and kept it in his Bible. Then he went towards the operating theatre and the anaesthetist injected his spine with anaesthetic and put too much in and he died. Yes – it was a mistake but it happened. They tried to resuscitate him; they tried pumping his chest to get him to breathe again. The surgeon even climbed up onto his body and pushed his knees into his chest but it was no use. They watched the monitor of his heartbeat and it was level.

So they went out to the wife who was waiting outside and said, "We're very sorry, but we've lost him." She said, "No you haven't! Go back and try again." She was quite a little woman but she had a strong faith and a lot of courage. She told them, "Go back in and try again." So they went back in and tried again and nothing happened. She refused to accept it. So they put him in a bed with a mechanical pump to his lungs to help him breathe, a mechanical thing on his heart to keep his heart pumping, but his brain was dead and they could get no response in his brain.

Now that is clinical death. They could have signed a death certificate, but because of that little woman they kept him going on the machines for ten days. Then she came in to visit him and he was gone. She said, "Where's my husband?" They said, "We needed his organs for transplanting and you did say we could have them. So we've switched the machines off and taken him to the morgue." This little woman said, "Bring him back! Bring him back!" So they brought him back and hooked him up again at which point he opened his eyes and looked at them. He saw this little paper on the floor that he had written, and he nodded his head as much to say, "Pick that up." They picked it up and read, "I go to sleep and I wake up, because the Lord is with me." Well he became called the "miracle boy" of that centre which was the famous Stanford Medical Center in the States.

They finally left him alone in the room and he thought, "The operation has been a success. I have no pain." He got out of bed but he had to unhook a bottle that was feeding his arm, and he got out of bed. He walked up and down the bedroom and he said, "The pain is gone. The operation has taken away the growth." A nurse came into the room and she shrieked at him and said, "Get back into the bed!" He said, "But I'm all right! I can walk!" A few days later he walked out of that hospital without the bottle feeding him because now he could feed himself. The nurses and doctors lined the whole passage and were cheering the miracle man as he left.

I have seen the medical records of it, but he came back to his old body. He is still alive but he will die again because that is not resurrection. Resurrection is re-creation; resurrection is a new body. Jesus will never die again. Lazarus died again, the widow of Nain's son died again – that is coming back to life. But Jesus didn't come back to life he went on to life. As I have asked before: where do you think Jesus got his resurrection clothes from? Have you thought about that? The God who made a new body for him gave him new clothes at the same time, and you will have clothes in heaven because God will make those for your new body. My new body is going to be just like his glorious body, and when you are in your eighties you can't wait to be thirty-three again! I am looking forward to that.

The resurrection is the central fact of Jesus' uniqueness; nobody before or since has ever – not come back to life, but gone on to a new life with a new body. That is why he is called the firstborn of all creation. That is why we worship on a Sunday because it is the beginning of God's new creation.

We remember two unique things about his ascension, which took place two months later. First, Jesus left this world two months after he died. I don't know of anybody else who has done that, do you? Most people leave this world the day they die. But Jesus stayed around for two months and then he left.

Furthermore, he took his body with him. All other people

leave it behind. Mohammed is dead, Confucius is dead, Buddha is dead, and you can visit their tombs. But Jesus is alive. That is why there is an empty one, but there is no shrine where you can go and worship the dead Saviour. That is the difference – he is unique; there is no one like him. That is why we can never mix our faith with other religions.

Here are two final comments. The first is that the Christian faith is *exclusive*. Like Christ, it is unique. Christianity is Christ and therefore it is exclusive. We can never consider the idea of mixing our faith with other faiths. We may have to pay a heavy price for that stance as the religions of the world come together, but nevertheless it is exclusive and you can't mix truth with error. There is no other name under heaven by which a person can be saved except the name of Jesus. But by the same token our faith is *inclusive*. It must be for everybody. Those two things go together.

Exclusive faith must be inclusive. If it is the only way then everybody has a right to hear it and we have a right to tell them, we have a duty to share it with them. That is why Christianity must be a missionary religion, an evangelising religion. When we have found such a salvation it is our solemn duty to go and share it with those who need it, however offensive that may be.

One of the pressures that will come upon us is a law forbidding proselytising, as they call it. It will not be long before we are forbidden to try to convert someone of another faith to ours. There are already countries where that law is in operation but we have no choice. We can't help it. Our Jesus tells us to go and make disciples of all the nations and we have got a duty to tell them he is alive for evermore, that he will judge everybody on earth, and that he is coming again to rule this world until the kingdoms of this world become the kingdoms of our God and of his Christ. Amen.

ABOUT DAVID PAWSON

A speaker and author with uncompromising faithfulness to the Holy Scriptures, David brings clarity and a message of urgency to Christians to uncover hidden treasures in God's Word.

Born in England in 1930, David began his career with a degree in Agriculture from Durham University. When God intervened and called him to become a Minister, he completed an MA in Theology at Cambridge University and served as a Chaplain in the Royal Air Force for three years. He moved on to pastor several churches, including the Millmead Centre in Guildford, which became a model for many UK church leaders. In 1979, the Lord led him into an international ministry. His current itinerant ministry is predominantly to church leaders. David and his wife Enid currently reside in the county of Hampshire in the UK.

Over the years, he has written a large number of books, booklets, and daily reading notes. His extensive and very accessible overviews of the books of the Bible have been published and recorded in *Unlocking the Bible*. Millions of copies of his teachings have been distributed in more than 120 countries, providing a solid biblical foundation.

He is reputed to be the "most influential Western preacher in China" through the broadcast of his best-selling *Unlocking the Bible* series into every Chinese province by Good TV. In the UK, David's teachings are often broadcast on Revelation TV.

Countless believers worldwide have also benefited from his generous decision in 2011 to make available his extensive audio video teaching library free of charge at www.davidpawson.org and we have recently uploaded all of David's video to a dedicated channel on www.youtube.com

THE EXPLAINING SERIES
BIBLICAL TRUTHS SIMPLY EXPLAINED

If you have been blessed reading this book, there are more available in the series. Please register to download more booklets for free by visiting
www.explainingbiblicaltruth.global

Other booklets in the *Explaining* series will include:
The Amazing Story of Jesus
The Resurrection: *The Heart of Christianity*
Studying the Bible
Being Anointed and Filled with the Holy Spirit
New Testament Baptism
How to study a book of the Bible: Jude
The Key Steps to Becoming a Christian
What the Bible says about Money
What the Bible says about Work
Grace – *Undeserved Favour, Irresistible Force or Unconditional Forgiveness?*
Eternally secure? – *What the Bible says about being saved*
De-Greecing the Church – The impact of Greek thinking on Christian beliefs
Three texts often taken out of context: *Expounding the truth and exposing error*
The Trinity
The Truth about Christmas

They will also be avaiable to purchase as print copies from:
Amazon or **www.thebookdepository.com**

UNLOCKING THE BIBLE

A unique overview of both the Old and New Testaments, from internationally acclaimed evangelical speaker and author David Pawson. *Unlocking the Bible* opens up the Word of God in a fresh and powerful way. Avoiding the small detail of verse by verse studies, it sets out the epic story of God and his people in Israel. The culture, historical background and people are introduced and the teaching applied to the modern world. Eight volumes have been brought into one compact and easy to use guide to cover both the Old and New Testaments in one massive omnibus edition. *The Old Testament: The Maker's Instructions* (The five books of law); *A Land and A Kingdom* (Joshua, Judges, Ruth, 1&2 Samuel, 1&2 Kings); *Poems of Worship and Wisdom* (Psalms, Song of Solomon, Proverbs, Ecclesiastes, Job); *Decline and Fall of an Empire* (Isaiah, Jeremiah and other prophets); *The Struggle to Survive* (Chronicles and prophets of exile); *The New Testament: The Hinge of History* (Mathew, Mark, Luke, John and Acts); *The Thirteenth Apostle* (Paul and his letters); *Through Suffering to Glory* (Hebrews, the letters of James, Peter and Jude, the Book of Revelation). Already an international bestseller.

JESUS: THE SEVEN WONDERS OF HISTORY

This book is the result of a lifetime of telling 'the greatest story ever told' around the world. David re-told it to many hundreds of young people in Kansas City, USA, who heard it with uninhibited enthusiasm, 'tweeting' on the internet about 'this cute old English gentleman' even while he was speaking.

Taking the middle section of the Apostles' Creed as a framework, David explains the fundamental facts about Jesus on which the Christian faith is based in a fresh and stimulating way. Both old and new Christians will benefit from this 'back to basics' call and find themselves falling in love with their Lord all over again.

OTHER TEACHINGS
BY DAVID PAWSON

For the most up to date list of David's Books
go to: **www.davidpawsonbooks.com**

To purchase David's Teachings
go to: **www.davidpawson.com**

www.ingramcontent.com/pod-product-compliance
Lightning Source LLC
Chambersburg PA
CBHW070119110526
44587CB00016BA/2724